Sports Illustrated KIDS

★ HOCKEY SUPERSTARS ★

PHIL KESSEL

BY MATT DOEDEN

CAPSTONE PRESS
a capstone imprint

Sports Illustrated Kids Hockey Superstars are published by Capstone Press, 1710 Roe Crest Drive, North Mankato, Minnesota 56003.
www.capstonepub.com

Library of Congress Cataloging-in-Publication Data
Doeden, Matt.
  Phil Kessel / by Matt Doeden.
      pages cm. — (Sports illustrated kids. Hockey superstars)
  Includes bibliographical references and index.
  Summary: "Details the life and career of hockey superstar Phil Kessel"—Provided by publisher.
  ISBN 978-1-4296-8278-7 (library binding)
  ISBN 978-1-4914-9022-8 (paperback)
  ISBN 978-1-4914-7603-1 (eBook PDF)
1. Kessel, Phil, 1987—Juvenile literature. 2. Hockey players—United States—Biography—Juvenile literature. 3. Hockey players—Canada—Biography—Juvenile literature. I. Title.
  GV848.5.K45D64 2016
  796.962092—dc23
  [B]   2015006651

Editorial Credits
Brenda Haugen, editor; Terri Poburka, designer; Eric Gohl, media researcher; Tori Abraham, production specialist

Photo Credits
Dreamstime: Jerry Coli, 21; Getty Images: Bruce Bennett, 8, Jim McIsaac, 10, Jonathan Nackstrand, 4, Martin Rose, 6–7, NHLI/Jonathan Kozub, 1, NHLI/Steve Babineau, 16; Newscom: Cal Sport Media/Andy Blenkush, 11, Cal Sport Media/Anthony Nesmith, 23, Icon SMI/David Stluka, 9, Icon SMI/Keith Hamilton, cover, Reuters/Jim Young, 25, USA Today Sports/Adam Hunger, 26, USA Today Sports/Tom Szczerbowski, 29; Sports Illustrated: Damian Strohmeyer, 13, 18–19, 30–31 (background), 32 (background), David E. Klutho, 14
Design Elements: Shutterstock

Source Note
Page 15, line 9: Associated Press. "Bruins rookie coming to terms with cancer diagnosis" ESPN NHL. 2006 Dec. 17. 2015 March 14. http://sports.espn.go.com/nhl/news/story?id=2699737

Printed in the United States of America in North Mankato, Minnesota.
032015   008823CGF15

TABLE OF CONTENTS

CHAPTER 1

TAKING CONTROL

The U.S. men's hockey team was coming off a huge win. They had just beaten Russia in the **preliminary round** of the 2014 Winter Olympics. They could earn a **bye** in the medal round with a win over their next opponent, Slovenia.

Team USA **winger** Phil Kessel was one of the most dangerous goal-scorers in the world. He took the ice on a mission. Just a minute into the game, Kessel skated through Slovenia's defense. He dodged a defender, then fired a shot into the net. 1-0 USA!

preliminary round—the games played to decide which teams will play in the medal round

bye—when a team has played well enough to automatically advance to the second round of the playoffs

winger—a type of forward who usually stays near the sides of the zone

Less than three minutes later, Kessel was at it again.
He was near Slovenia's goal when **center** Joe Pavelski slid a
pass his way. Kessel grabbed the puck and jabbed it in for his
second goal.

The United States was in control. Kessel helped seal the
deal in the second period. He collected a rebound near
the goal and popped it into the net. It was his third goal

of the game. He'd just completed one of hockey's greatest feats, a **hat trick**! Kessel was the first American in more than a decade to score a hat trick in an Olympic hockey game. Team USA cruised to a 5-1 victory and into the knockout round.

center—the player who participates in a face-off at the beginning of play

hat trick—when a player scores three goals in one game

CHAPTER 2

AMATEUR STAR

Philip Joseph Kessel Jr. grew up in a family of athletes. He was born October 2, 1987, in Madison, Wisconsin. His father, Phil Sr., had been a star football quarterback in college. His mother, Kathy, ran track in college. But the game of choice for Phil Jr. and his siblings, Blake and Amanda, was hockey.

Madison was a good place for a young hockey player. It has a strong youth hockey tradition. It's also the home of the University of Wisconsin, which has one of the top college hockey programs in the nation. Starting at age 7, Phil played for a youth team called the Madison Capitols. His speed and sharp shooting made him the team's star.

FAST FACT

The Madison Capitols were coached by Bob Suter. He was famous for being a member of the 1980 U.S. Olympic hockey team that shocked the world by winning the gold medal.

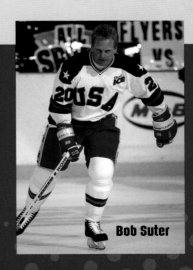

Bob Suter

The Kohl Center is home to the University of Wisconsin hockey teams.

Kessel was dominating junior hockey by the time he was 14. During the 2001–02 season, he scored 176 goals and had 110 assists in 86 games. That added up to 286 total points and a jaw-dropping average of 3.3 points per game!

Two years later Kessel left Madison and moved to Ann Arbor, Michigan. In Ann Arbor he played with the

SUPERSTAR SISTER

Phil isn't the only member of the Kessel family to earn hockey fame. His younger sister, Amanda, is also a star. As a kid Amanda played for the Capitols' boys team. She later led her high school's team to two under-19 national championships.

Amanda accepted a **scholarship** to play college hockey for the University of Minnesota Golden Gophers. She

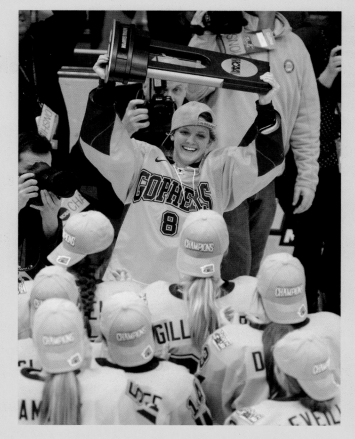

scored two goals and added two assists in her first game! She led the Gophers to national championships in 2012 and 2013. She also earned a silver medal at the 2014 Winter Olympics.

U.S. National Team Development Program. He was a star. Kessel led Team USA to the World Under-18 Championship in 2005. In the team's six tournament games, Kessel had 9 goals and 16 points.

scholarship—money given to a student to pay for school

National Hockey League (NHL) scouts were noticing Kessel. Some compared him to Sidney Crosby, an amazing NHL **prospect** in Canada. But Kessel was too young to enter the 2005 NHL **Draft**. He accepted a scholarship to play for the University of Minnesota Golden Gophers.

Kessel had a good season for Minnesota. He scored 18 goals and helped the Gophers win the Western Collegiate Hockey Association (WCHA) championship. He was also named the WCHA **Rookie** of the Year. That made him one of the top prospects in the 2006 draft. The Boston Bruins selected him fifth overall. Kessel signed a three-year contract to join the Bruins.

prospect—a person who is likely to play pro hockey

draft—the process of choosing a person to join a sports organization or team

rookie—a first-year player

CHAPTER 3

THE NHL

Kessel quickly impressed his coaches in Boston. He made his NHL **debut** in October 2006. Six games later he scored his first NHL goal.

But his focus soon shifted. Kessel wasn't feeling well. He had found a small lump on one of his testicles. Doctors gave him the bad news. Kessel had cancer.

"I couldn't believe it," Kessel said. "It was tough. I had a hard time with it."

Kessel left the team in December to receive treatment and was gone for several weeks. Doctors removed the tumor. They had good news. The cancer had not spread, and it was unlikely to return.

shoot-out—a method of breaking a tie score at the end of overtime play

debut—a player's first game

Kessel returned to the Bruins in January. Although he struggled after his recovery, he was chosen to play in the 2007 NHL YoungStars Game. Kessel showed off his talent by scoring a hat trick, including the game-winning goal.

Kessel was much improved in 2007–08. He tallied his first NHL hat trick October 12. For the season he scored 19 goals and helped the Bruins reach the playoffs. Kessel was one of Boston's few bright spots in the playoff series. He scored three goals. But the Montreal Canadiens beat Boston in the first round four games to three.

FAST FACT

Kessel was honored after the 2006–07 season with the Bill Masterton Memorial Trophy. This annual honor goes to an NHL player for "qualities of perseverance and sportsmanship."

perseverance—to keep doing something in spite of difficulties

The Bruins enjoyed a great 2008–09 regular season. Kessel came out on fire. He scored six goals in the team's first six games. His 36 goals for the season led the Bruins. Boston earned the top playoff seed in the Eastern Conference.

Boston again faced Montreal in the opening round. This time the Bruins were in charge. Despite an injured

shoulder, Kessel scored four goals as the Bruins swept the Canadiens.

The Bruins then faced the Carolina Hurricanes. It was a back-and-forth battle. Kessel had a key assist on the goal that forced overtime in Game 7. But it wasn't enough. Carolina scored in overtime and ended Boston's season.

The 2009 off-season was hectic for the 22-year-old Kessel. It started with surgery on his injured shoulder. Meanwhile Kessel and the Bruins tried to work out a new contract. After talks broke down, the Bruins traded Kessel to the Toronto Maple Leafs.

Kessel missed about a month of regular season games as he recovered from his shoulder surgery. It was a rough way to start with his new team. But Kessel managed to score 30 or more goals in each of his first three seasons with Toronto. The team struggled, though, missing the playoffs all three times.

FAST FACT

Kessel was a member of Team USA at the 2010 Winter Olympics in Vancouver, British Columbia, Canada. He earned a silver medal when Canada beat Team USA in a thrilling overtime gold-medal game.

Things finally started to turn around in 2012–13. Kessel caught fire at the end of the season. He scored 10 goals in the Maple Leafs' last 10 games. His play helped power the Leafs into the playoffs.

They faced the Bruins in the first round. Kessel played great against his old team. He scored four goals in the seven-game series. His play helped Toronto take a big lead in Game 7. But the Bruins staged an amazing comeback in the final minutes to win the game. Toronto's season was over.

HEARTBREAK

Game 7. Toronto vs. Boston. It was the deciding game, and everything was going right for the Maple Leafs. Early in the third period, Kessel banged in a goal for a 3-1 lead. Minutes later he added an assist to stretch the lead to 4-1. The game seemed like it was over. Kessel and his teammates were cruising toward the second round of the playoffs.

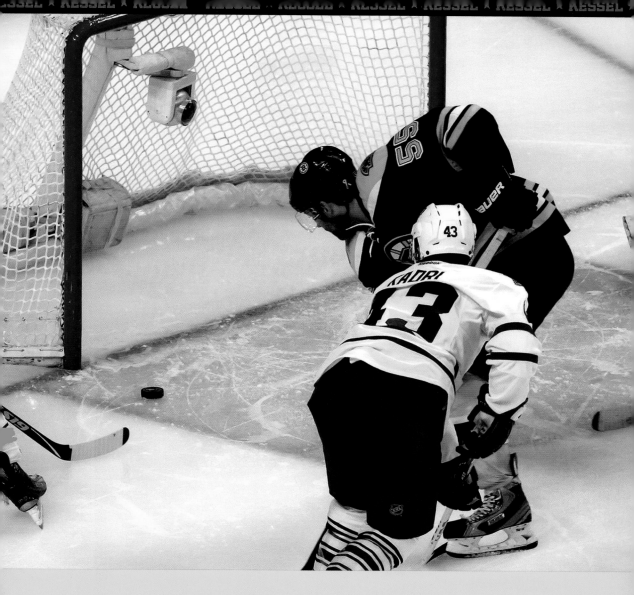

The Bruins scored a goal midway through the period. But the score stayed 4-2 with less than 90 seconds remaining. Then the unthinkable happened. The Bruins scored two goals in a stretch of 31 seconds! Yet another Boston goal in overtime sealed one of the most heartbreaking losses in NHL playoff history. No other team in NHL history had lost Game 7 after leading by three goals in the third period.

In February 2014 Kessel traveled with Team USA to Sochi, Russia, for the 2014 Winter Olympics. The Americans started out hot, winning all three games in the preliminary round. Kessel's hat trick against Slovenia was one of the highlights.

Kessel struck again in the medal round, scoring in a 5-2 win over the Czech Republic. Kessel and his teammates advanced to the semifinal game. But a 1-0 loss to Canada ended their gold medal dreams. Then the Americans lost the bronze-medal game 5-0 to Finland. Kessel finished the tournament with a total of five goals and three assists. He was named the tournament's best forward. But he and his teammates went home empty-handed.

FAST FACT

Kessel signed an eight-year contract with the Maple Leafs after the 2013 season. The contract pays him an average of $8 million per season.

Kessel returned to Toronto. The Maple Leafs were in the thick of the Eastern Conference playoff chase. But Kessel and the team went into a slump. The Leafs lost 16 of their last 22 games, including 12 of their final 14. Once again they were left out of the playoff picture.

Toronto fans and reporters were growing restless by 2015. The team was in the middle of a rough patch. Many of the negative comments centered on captain Dion Phaneuf. By March, Kessel had heard enough. He came to Phaneuf's defense by blasting the Toronto media. It was one way of showing that Kessel was taking a bigger leadership role than ever before.

FAST FACT

In November and December of 2008, Kessel scored at least one point in 18 straight games. That's tied for the most in history by an American-born player.

CHAPTER 4

THE FUTURE

Phil Kessel made himself a star with his amazing performance at the 2014 Winter Olympics. He has also shined in the few chances he's had to play on the NHL playoff stage. But it hasn't been enough. He's only been to the playoffs one time with Toronto and has yet to lead the Leafs to the **Stanley Cup**.

There's no denying Kessel's raw talent. He's an elite goal-scorer and a major threat every time he steps onto the ice. Fans are eager for Kessel and his team to take the next steps. A deep playoff run will help cement Kessel's place as one of the NHL's biggest stars.

Stanley Cup—the trophy given each year to the NHL champion

FAST FACT

Kessel was named to his third NHL All-Star Game in 2015. He was also chosen as an NHL All-Star in 2011 and 2012.

GLOSSARY

bye (BY)—when a team has played well enough to automatically advance to the second round of the playoffs

center (SEN-tur)—the player who participates in a face-off at the beginning of play

debut (DAY-byoo)—a player's first game

draft (DRAFT)—the process of choosing a person to join a sports organization or team

hat trick (HAT TRIK)—a feat achieved by a hockey player who scores three goals in one game

perseverance (per-suh-VEER-uhns)—to keep doing something in spite of difficulties

preliminary round (pree-LIM-uh-nah-ree ROWND)—the games played to decide which teams will advance to the medal round

prospect (PRAHS-pekt)—a person who is likely to play pro hockey

rookie (RUK-ee)—a first-year player

scholarship (SKOL-ur-ship)—money to pay education expenses

shoot-out (SHOOT-owt)—a method of breaking a tie score at the end of overtime play

Stanley Cup (STAN-lee KUP)—the trophy given each year to the NHL champion

winger (WING-ur)—a type of forward who usually stays near the sides of the zone

READ MORE

Doeden, Matt. *Sidney Crosby: Hockey Superstar.* Sports Illustrated Kids: Superstar Athletes. North Mankato, Minn.: Capstone Press, 2012.

Frederick, Shane. *Six Degrees of Sidney Crosby: Connecting Hockey Stars.* Sports Illustrated Kids: Six Degrees of Sports. North Mankato, Minn.: Capstone Press, 2015.

Gitlin, Marty. *Hockey.* Best Sport Ever. Minneapolis: ABDO Pub., 2012.

INTERNET SITES

FactHound offers a safe, fun way to find Internet sites related to this book. All of the sites on FactHound have been researched by our staff.

Here's all you do:

Visit *www.facthound.com*

Type in this code: 9781429682787

 Check out projects, games and lots more at
www.capstonekids.com

INDEX